P9-AQB-094

On the Other Side of the World

by
Michèle Kahn
illustrated by Ye Xin

This edition is published by special arrangement with Bordas.

Grateful acknowledgment is made to Bordas, Paris, France, for permission to reprint *The Other Side of the World* by Michèle Kahn, illustrated by Ye Xin. © 1987 by Bordas. Originally published in France under the title *L'autre bout du monde*.

Printed in the United States of America

ISBN 0-15-302123-3

4 5 6 7 8 9 10 035 97 96 95

On the Other Side of the World

by
Michèle Kahn
illustrated by Ye Xin

HARCOURT BRACE & COMPANY
Orlando Atlanta Austin Boston San Francisco Chicago Dallas New York
Toronto London

Every night Ana Maria says,
"Mama, tell me a story.
Tell me a story please."

Then her mother begins,
As you know, the Earth is round,
round like a ball.
On the other side of the world,
there is a country called Japan.
And in Japan there lives a boy.

He is just as old as you.

And he likes to play with a ball,
just as you do.

Did you know that when it is day here,

it is night there?

When it is time for dinner,
I say to you,
"Come, sit in the chair."

The boy's mama says,
"Come, sit on the mat."
Then she gives him his dinner
on a very low table.

When you are eating
with a spoon and a fork,

the boy in Japan is eating
with chopsticks.

In your house, you wear slippers.

In Japan, they go around
the house in their socks.
They take off their shoes
at the door.

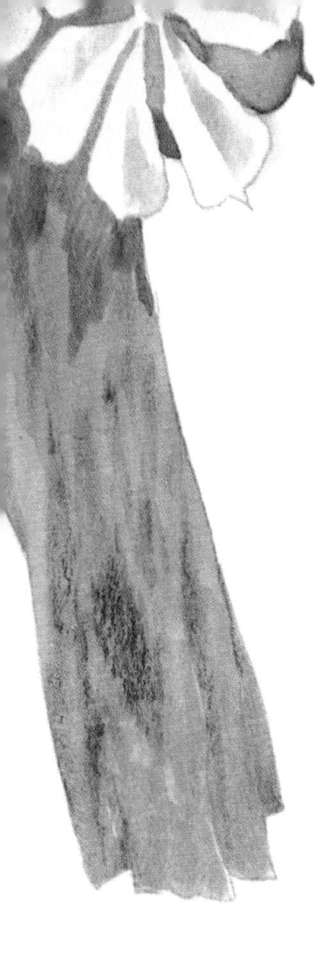

Here, as a tree
gets older,
it grows
taller
and taller.

Our friends in Japan have
a pine tree in their house.
It is forty years old.
But it is still smaller than the boy.
A tiny tree like this is a bonsai tree.

When you go to a party,
you may wear your best clothes.

In Japan, children may wear
their best kimonos to a party.

You put letters together to make words.
You use a pen or a pencil to write.

Sometimes your friend
uses a brush to write.
When he does,
his words look like drawings.
They are very pretty.

When you take a bath,
you get into the tub first.
Then you wash with soap and
rinse off.

In Japan, people wash with soap
and rinse off first.
Then, they get into the tub.

At night I come to your bed.
I say good night
and give you a kiss.

In Japan the boy's mama kneels
by his mattress on the floor.
"Now where is that boy of mine?"
she asks.
"Oh! He's hiding under
the blanket!"

Do you know what your friend says
before he goes to sleep?
I think you can guess!
The boy in Japan says,
"Mama, please tell me a story."

Then his mother begins,
"As you know, the Earth is round,
round like a ball.
On the other side of the world,
there is a country.
And in that country there lives a girl.
She is just as old as you.
And when she goes to bed,
she says, just as you do,
'Mama, please tell me a story.'"